the goddess of greed

(one that be square)

sort of a introduction

tuesday

nice looking woman

starbucks

fucked up arm

like her

my girl

it is my daughter

coming out of nowhere

looking for me

why

why did she not solve

her life

and here i see her

a total fuck up

good mother

whore in the end

do not want to contend

it is all animal

need to think about it

the things in myself

totally beautiful

so in love with them

tears of sadness

of late

for both my children

both a fucked up wreck

don't understand

don't even understand

that they even want me around

the situation is acute

in car

need fucking

WOMAN!!!!

my life

trying to be okay

you need woman

but

they say fuck you

(it is important to know

you touch her there

and she is yours

even if you

fucking

i don't know what??)

these fuck head people

they don't know love

they practice with

their big cocks

and just get tired

the woman

loves even more

even if it is a

waste of time

i am not blaming women

i guess i am

and i never have

the reason

is she loses

everything when

you fuck her up

like i just did

because she only

knows love

so i retract the statement

going to get into

trouble now with

myself

my little ones

men

we only know life

we need love

like you cannot believe

another thing i should

not say about men

so i retract that too

realize

privacy

these are my personal

so i curse you

in a playful way

that you do not remember

thoughts

starbucks

nice woman her

with fucked up arm...

could heal her

if she were to let me

fuck

her

***

accuracy

don't bother

tips to a long future

look to it

be at work

fuck it

go to the street!

accentuation

learn to eat

we need to figure

out where to get food

so think about it

little farms

cool

realize

ulimate

mass exit to the street

when the cars go

we do not want them

***

will check out this girl

it is pretty useless

have feeling

she is with someone

they always get with

someone

the men

just jump on them

need for love

and then

they fuck it up

none of my business

basically

i am just a writer

don't have the feel for poetry

like to talk

NEED WOMAN!!!!

anywa

sliding in and out of

bullshit

it is getting better

please buy

try paperback

cool

anything

i am poor

homeless

like a fucking nothing

please buy

me

for my

effort

please

i give

you do shit

at least give me money

cunts...

i mean that in a nice way

***

gonna get cigarette

bad day

fuck you

just playing

i do not want to struggle

books get worse

and you need them

lessons

life is for learning

not school shit

don't get personal

do not shoot others

because

guns

are

available

and they look like toys

fuckups

don't want to know you

total fuckups

killing others

because

you can use a GUN

***

so fucking angry

***

hi liero

want to go and pick up my
daughter

from lisa

tomorrow

i need a hundred for gas

that is all i am asking of you

after that you

are a fuck up

my girls

are easing up on me

it is good

but it is rage for them

i tell them why

they are more important

to me that anything

girls that time finds

us empty

we will be of

and then to

and finished thereof

so to them

we accede the county of fine

so to country demolished

what do we care

rage follows

that in time

we find the need

for pussy

unwind

open your legs

and forget

the day is blind

to each the time

we need food

so open your legs

and forget

to find the time

for money

wild

the little girl

blind

so to the end

we go

and more

and fuck her some

more

the end of blind

to be kind

to her the nice

child

stop

interfering with me

it is distraught

but this is exactly

what i wanted

so to little girl

in there with open legs

and they go off

on me

***

I AM HAPPY

***

poem

arm fucked

hair pretty

so good looking

be yourself

and love another

***

good poem

my girls

are in top form

challenging me

it is life

as you warm it

and they have words

to the hilt

gave that poem

to that girl

she is good

now

so to thought

of them

thanks

need help

in degree

not to help of not

so they inflect

and their answer

is of be...??

that's pretty good

explain

no

and it is regular

and i have to look

the verb

is
of be

as is to be

love

(repeat a million times

it stays steady

eternal love)

((a continues sentence))

verb

as is to be action please

to be action of please

as action is

to long sentence

verb

redundant

be to any sentence

be long

to be

(another circular sentence

of love

can be repeated to whatever)

((a sentence of longing))

baby

that nail in the coffin

that please

to be baby

(don't want to know)

the goddess of greed

new title

that degree be

in silence of

the degree to be

neglect

as woman

is to be woman

of degree

that say to woman all

then in degree of woman be

the degree of

then woman be

pregnant with child

that in earning of

that degree of to make

child

the degree of man

love

then to be man

of degree that love

of another find

then degree of find

to make love

then to of that degree

to tell the degree

to

many children

(stop

i am getting emotional)

to thought that make

the same of same

to same that be

then same to be

as verb same

any word can be

so in love with thee

we are

your little ones

(i am really emotional
now)

i answer
in same of women swim
that in seed we find

i love you very much
you now steady me

and love free

i see it already

(now they

are

emotional)

thoughts to perfection

(protect the planet)

is that what a woman is about

a big cock

it is pretty shameful

that she does not know

how to love anymore

and we must go alone

i am in such pain and hurt

it is unbelievable

i can't even write

i am sure that a woman

is a good thing

i am back home

it was a horrible

couple of days

that woman

is on my mind

i can go back there

she said i had a home

at her place

i have written so

many books

of course

it is much more

difficult to read

than write

so that is okay

how can i make it easy

i probably haven't

i sense things

i sense meaning

that is how i get my writing

it is not easy

and makes me very tired

so i am very tired

i am in the car

i realize

that my brother

had the spare key all the time

so this is not a nice thing

he wants to take my car

and give me a van

he has not asked me

i am pretty sure

he wants to give it back

to his daughter

and i understand

that the now

restraining order

is on both my sister's house

and his

and the restaurant

this is all pretty fantastic

i guess i am a good writer

but i am not a good

human being

not only do i have

trouble with god bothering

me my family

does not much like me

so i am going

to leave them

these words sound off

give me a minute

i keep on asking

the lord god to leave

he never does

he refuses

i ask him

and this is so unfair

because he

interferes

he does not care that

he interferes

we are supposed to

be nice to each other

and i am helping him

but he just wants

to flat out kill me

it will be interesting

when i die

i am sure he will be

waiting for me

so i will not die

also he is berating

parts of me to suicide

this is the lord god

he has a bug up the ass

he also does

not want me to have a

girlfriend

he is intensely stupid

but i am unravelling

things

and it will pretty much

go away

he is inside of me

and keeps asking for food

this is a form of possession

and i tell him no food

and he takes it anyway

it is so insane

it is not even funny

i do all this stuff despite

because i am a good person

i need a female

and the computer

is almost out of charge

it is a little bit late

i believe i killed someone

the god of this place

it was not much

he was bugging me

so i cut his head off

and dumped it

and his body

at his wife's house

he was useless

always bothering me

i am now in the burger place

i am very tired

it is not a bad place this

i like it

i have no money

but i might have

so i am going to try

i want to get a coke

i buy a coke

there seem to be others

in there

in my body

so let us discuss

is there anybody

in my body that should

not be there

i ask

is there a yes

okay

you had better go

or i will chop your heads

off

and send you home

i am in the mood

i guess i have to

so i go have a cigarette

and come back fulfilled

i love my ladies

they are all to me

there is a lot of blood

all over the place

it was fun

you cannot come into a body

you will get your head

chopped off

and spat out

where you will be

no one will know

and nobody will miss you

because you are an idiot

to take a chance

with your life

in any way at all

congratulations

you are all dead now

i am drinking my coke

this computer

for some reason

it will not charge

it is an old computer

it is not too good

and the cord my brother

got me does not work

too well

so

it is not going to work

i am going to have to start

working out of the library

i will save this

i don't know

it might work for a while

i just need to get another

cord

i can do it myself

i need to get a job

i need to find a lady

and have some babies

very tired not

going to go and sleep in car

it is a little later

i am not feeling too good

i am a healer of things

i don't know

if you understand this

some of us do

if you do

it is good for you

try

i would like to see more

healers

if you believe

you can do it

in a good way

only keep it for yourself

imagination

i think it is very important

to heal yourself

in that way

because to stay a good

person

you will need it

there are things

around us that do not

want us here

we must protect ourselves

you do this by thinking

and saying exact words

always try to keep to

your exact words

if you go wrong

do not worry

in a way

things keep together

you must not

really worry about it

the thing is we are not harmed

but we are caused to be harmed

they cannot come here and

do it directly

we hope

but we are definitely hated

it is getting worse

because they are

in a panic of being found out

we go now to do it

to report them

on this earth

where we are

we ask for help

there are those that

want us dead

anyway they can

we are human

human beings

and are just trying

to get by

there are a lot of good ones

here

they want to say

we deserve it

because they practice pain

and serve themselves

only

i repeat there

is a conspiracy

to ruin planets

and bring the planets

down

so i ask attention

to be placed with us

to return to us

and take care of this problem

those in charge

of us are responsible

for many crimes

it is spreading and getting worse

so i take a hand

and do it all myself

so done

sitting in parking lot

computer useless

library

tomorrow sunday

good day

thoughts

it is cold in car

we all have to

get out at once

all to the street

and take it over

with freedom

thought one

children on the street

look after them

the thought is

why can't we have

children on the street

protect it

that was thought two

thought three

arewe built for war

or fighting

our bodies do not look

like it

the hands hold things

it is not a fist

unravel your bodies

to it's true meaning

and purpose

do not accept influence

it is to interfere

with your mind

these thoughts

go quickly

realize we are in trouble

sex on everybody's mind

while chance slips past

i am not to inform

you must do these things

yourselves

if you love life

i live in a car

what's wrong

with living in a car

is a house expensive

where does all that money go

i need a child

fuck them

thought any

close to war

surrender

and to war no

emblem

of fortitude

wasted

and that is about it

lots to type

and you are lazy

i cannot fuck your

woman for you

so do not tell me

need to start

walking

i am fucking alone

remember

words are harmless

that's the big one

words are harmless

they do not have

to mean anything

that is why there

should be no law

thought

of the day...

words are worthless

in a way

to say

to say

the recognition of

another

thought of the day...

no more thoghts

tired

brain will not

even work

sleep

i know the truth

so i am happier

than most

so know the truth

but do not

think

i have a woman

friend to be

that to be

biggest thought

(protect the planet)

strange that subject be

sitting on a tree

an old lady fornicating

with wood

saying she is not happy

man comes out

some kind of attack

was made on me back

there

i disappear

that light we right

to light switch off

electricity gone

to song of repair

earth

to melody made

tu tu tere

we are gone

song follows

we are gone

to blue daffodils

to make the song

of repair

we open it all up

cracking the ground

with machines

turning over all

the concrete to sand

make it happen

machines disassemble

with delight

crack the sound

of metal

do not burn

any trees

crackle might

((might as well go

panhandle

it is almost

midnight

can't go to car

***

it is not big enough

that degree of

and i will leave this one small

and try the outrage

first part